Christian Philanthropy

Christian Philanthropy

Daily Devotions in Titus 2–3

Paul S. Jeon

RESOURCE *Publications* · Eugene, Oregon

CHRISTIAN PHILANTHROPY
Daily Devotions in Titus 2–3

Resource Publications
An Imprint of Wipf and Stock Publishers
199 W. 8th Ave., Suite 3
Eugene, OR 97401

www.wipfandstock.com

PAPERBACK ISBN: 978-1-5326-8112-7
HARDCOVER ISBN: 978-1-5326-8113-4
EBOOK ISBN: 978-1-5326-8114-1

Manufactured in the U.S.A.   APRIL 4, 2019

To Bora & Paul,
Trailblazers in doing good

Contents

Acknowledgments

First, I thank Brian Forman, a dear friend who strives to devote himself to good works. Second, I thank Paul and Bora Jin. They have touched so many lives in such profound ways and have left behind such a rich spiritual legacy for their children. Finally, I thank God for my parents who have made every attempt to live all of life for God.

Series Introduction

THIS SHORT BOOK ON the last two chapters of Titus is the second installment in this devotional series. I wrote it because I love the members of NewCity, the church where I serve as the lead pastor. As a church, we have adopted a simple philosophy toward ministry.[1] Our main ask from our members is that they would attend Sunday service regularly, fully commit to a small group, serve in one substantial way, and be purposeful about pursuing relationships with unbelievers.[2] This means that we have sought to weed out many good activities that might take away focus, time, and energy from these basic commitments—even "programs" like prayer meetings and Bible studies during the week.[3] Moreover, at NewCity we believe in the priority of fulfilling our most basic roles. In particular, we encourage men to aspire to become loving husbands and present fathers who achieve quality time through quantity time. This is impossible to do if they're spending the majority of their weekday evenings on church activities.

This ministry arrangement can create somewhat of a gap in biblical instruction. For this reason, we encourage our members

1. This is based on a myriad of books, including *Simple Church*, *Essentialism*, *Unstuck Church*, and *Deep Work*.

2. We also teach our members to tithe and pursue generous lives. I am currently writing a short book on what I dub as "a sustainable but fruitful approach to discipleship."

3. To be clear, I am not suggesting that a church should not engage in such activities during the week. This is the decision we have made given our "crazy busy" (DeYoung) culture and our desire to avoid the trap of doing so much but accomplishing so little. Other churches might conclude that these activities accord with their ministry philosophy.

to try to read the entire Bible in the course of a year or two and to nurture their devotional life. The kind of devotional life I promote is based on Bible memorization. I ask our members to take a chunk of Scripture, usually a section that is focused on a single theme, to memorize it to the point of easy recollection, to digest it until it becomes part and parcel of who they are, and then to consider concrete ways to repent and pursue change.[4] This complementary process of Bible reading and Bible memorization allows for growth in terms of breadth and depth. I write this devotion for my church members, hoping that it will facilitate the latter.

A word on the topic. I came across Paul's Letter to Titus somewhat by accident. Prior to my doctorate studies, a mentor suggested that I select a very manageable dissertation that would guarantee graduation. He commented, "There are just too many ABDs out there (All but dissertation)." Hence, when one of my Ph.D. advisors asked during a doctorate seminar whether anyone would be interested in applying his unique approach to Paul's Letters to Titus, I jumped at the opportunity. All this is to say that my immersion into this profound letter was expedient and fairly thoughtless.

But in the providence of God, I learned much from applying my professor's "chiastic approach" and, more so, from my extensive meditation on the apostle's tough words.[5] In my brief book *True Faith*, I highlight what the apostle seems to highlight, namely that Christians are to consider whether they have truly converted by examining the presence or absence of good works in their lives. In a sense, verse 16 of the first chapter gets at the burden of the book, "God they [the false teachers] profess to know, but by their works they deny."[6] Then as now, there is no shortage of persons who have convinced themselves that they are followers of Christ. Paul, however, being a good pastor and therefore not wanting any

4. For an example of this approach, see my devotional *God's Wisdom for Making Peace*.

5. The book that grew out of my dissertation on Titus is entitled *To Exhort and Reprove*.

6. Unless specified, all translations of the Titus text are my own.

under his care to bank on empty assurance, challenges believers to examine whether their lifestyle accords with the faith they profess. As he highlights in this letter, no one is saved by his works; nevertheless, saving faith always results in good works.[7]

Still a theme that needed further development was that of good works, i.e., philanthropy. In particular I was struck in the Letter to Titus by the twin presentations of God as the ultimate Philanthropist (3:4) and God's people as those zealous for good works (2:14). Perhaps these images struck me so profoundly because they have been somewhat alien to my conservative upbringing, and even now do not seem to characterize many devout Christians. It seems as though Bonhoeffer's concern for "cheap grace" has been realized in our culture today where professing believers celebrate God's kindness in Jesus Christ but fail to live out their calling to do good to all.[8]

Tim Keller's book *Ministries of Mercy* forced me to look back at my church experience thus far and critically examine what was missing. Such scrutiny is especially important to me now that I serve as a lead pastor and therefore am seeking to create a culture at my church that conforms to the norms of the kingdom. But perhaps more influential have been my encounters with believers over the past ten years that broke the stereotype of being either orthodox in theology (at the expense of philanthropy) or active in seeking justice and helping the poor (at the expense of theology). These individuals and families displayed a profound commitment to both orthodoxy and philanthropy. This new "breed" of believers challenged me by their lifestyles to reread my Bible and identify gaps in my understanding of the Christian life. In part because of my upbringing and my particular seminary training, but mostly because of my own ignorance and sin, I had failed to see what Paul

---

7. For further reflections on this theme, see my comments in *True Faith*.

8. Bonhoeffer, *Cost of Discipleship*, 44–45: "Cheap grace is the preaching of forgiveness without requiring repentance, baptism without church discipline, communion without confession, absolution without personal confession. Cheap grace is grace without discipleship, grace without the cross, grace without Jesus Christ, living and incarnate."

makes so clear in Titus, namely that *confessional theology and a devotion to philanthropy must go hand-in-hand.*

I wrote this devotional with one aim in mind: to underscore what I have missed and neglected for too many years—a zeal for good works, a wholehearted devotion to philanthropy. Like many immigrant children, I had learned to pursue excellence and success in order to vindicate my parents' great sacrifice; I had learned to achieve a better life for myself and my children. But the call of the kingdom is broader and deeper. Having been redeemed by Christ and made members of his elect people, all believers are to abound in doing good to all people. If this devotional simply plants the idea that "Philanthropy should be a basic part of my life as a follower of Christ," then it has fulfilled its purpose. For the glory of God, may we aspire to overflow with good works as God's chosen people.

Brief Background on the Letter to Titus[1]

TITUS, A KEY EMISSARY for the apostle Paul, was serving among the believers in Crete. Crete itself had much to be desired. "One of the Cretans, a prophet of their own, said, 'Cretans are always liars, evil beasts, lazy gluttons'" (1:12 *ESV*). Thus, the need for godly leaders was important—but all the more because false teachers had infiltrated the ranks. Paul describes such persons as "insubordinate, empty-talkers and deceivers" (1:10 *ESV*) who love to appear godly but whose lives indicate otherwise (1:16). Given this turbulent context, Paul's concern was for Titus to "appoint elders in every town" prior to rejoining the apostle. The appointment of such elders and takes up most of the first chapter of the letter.

Already in the first few verses, however, Paul communicates his main burden, namely that the believers in Crete would grasp this basic reality: an embrace of the truth of the gospel must be coupled with a godly lifestyle (1:1). It's likely that Paul's gospel of "free grace" had—thankfully—begun to penetrate the minds of believers. Paul's gospel, which he later summarizes in 3:3–7, underscores that God saves wicked people not because of their righteousness or good works but because of his own mercy and kindness. Such a gospel understandably can lead to the belief that good works don't matter—that we can be indifferent to philanthropy—because we're saved by grace, not works. This, however, represents a misunderstanding of the *telos* (the purpose) of our

1. More background information can be found in my commentary *To Exhort and Reprove*.

salvation: God does not save *according to* good works but *unto* good works (2:14). The Cretan believers needed to be reminded of this nuance; hence, Paul begins the second chapter not with the exhortation to "teach sound doctrine," but "teach what accords with sound doctrine" (2:1). That is, he wants Titus to delineate for these young believers the sort of lifestyle that corresponds with the gospel (2:2–10).

A notable characteristic of this letter is Paul's use of "appearance" language: "the grace of God has appeared" (2:11); "the appearing of the glory of our great God and Savior, Jesus Christ" (2:13); "But when the graciousness and philanthropy of God our Savior appeared" (3:4). Paul uses this "appearance" language to ground his many commands in the new reality that has arisen through God's revelation of the Son. Instead of just telling believers how they should live, he wants them to understand why they should pursue the good. Theologians refer to this dynamic as the "indicative-imperative": because of what God has done in Christ, we are to live in this way. Specifically, this letter could be understood as an apologetic (a defense) for why the only manner of life fitting for God's redeemed people is one of philanthropy.

The third and final chapter of the letter teases out concrete applications for pursuing good and reiterates Paul's summons for believers to live admirable lives. Perhaps the most telling verse in this chapter is verse 8: ". . . so that those who have believed in God may be intentional about dedicating themselves to good works." Yes, Paul wants his audience to believe in and hold to the gospel of grace. But Paul seems equally concerned that they live a life that accords with their profession of faith.

Noteworthy is that such a life is never described in terms of doing "great things for a great God." Instead, the call to do good begins with the immediate and obvious needs around us. For the Cretan believers, this meant supplying the basic needs of Zenas and Apollos (3:13). The high call to philanthropy and the lofty language of the gospel can sometimes overwhelm a person. Thankfully, in this final chapter Paul presents a life marked by philanthropy in radically ordinary ways—respect for authority, a tamed tongue, and courtesy and concern for all people. Recovering our call to live a good life should not be confused with a summons to a radical life.[2]

2. Which in my estimation is foreign to the ethos of the Bible. God isn't expecting us to be "radical" but obedient to the ordinary and clear things he has called us to do. In doing such things, we will be "radical" in a culture that is obsessed with being extraordinary but failing in the ordinary aspects of the Christian life.

Day 1

Titus 2:11–14

An Introduction to Titus 2:11–14

WHEN I BEGAN WRITING this devotion, a man came to me to share a concern about his son. He himself was a very accomplished businessman, so he was delighted when his son expressed a desire to go into business to make a lot of money. But his delight quickly turned to alarm when it became clear that his son wanted to make money for the sole purpose of acquiring more instead of wanting to help others. When he encouraged his son to consider money in terms philanthropy, his son asked, "Why should I give my hard-earned money to others? Why can't I just buy nice things for myself?"

These are fair questions. I often ask similar questions to my liberal friends who—admirably—are very devoted to philanthropy (often much more so than conservative Christians). To be clear, I myself believe that all who profess Jesus Christ as Lord and the Savior of sinners should give themselves over to helping others. Jesus commanded, "Let your light shine before others, so that they may see your good works and give glory to your Father who is in heaven" (Matthew 5:16). So I align myself with my liberal friends who engage in regular philanthropy. My questions, however, are intended to make the point that we must be able to give some basis for telling others *why* they should do good. I remain perplexed that some continue to say, "No one has the right to tell others what to do," and then assert, "We should always do our best to help others." Why should we?

The apostle Paul gives such a basis in Titus 2:11–14 by summarizing how Christians view all of history. (Notice that verse 11 begins with the explanatory "For.") Your individual questions concerning ethics can only be answered when you ask the bigger question of what life is all about. If we suppose that tomorrow all life, as we know it, will come to an end because of a shooting comet, and if indeed there is no life after death, then the only sensible conclusion seems to be, "Let us eat and drink, for tomorrow we die" (1 Corinthians 15:32). But if life has meaning, because Christ has come and will come again, and if he came in large part to create a people "who are zealous for good works" (Titus 2:14), then the main pursuit of our lives should be to abound in good in order to glorify our God and Savior.

Prayer

Father in Heaven, thank you for your Word of truth that brings clarity to what matters in life and to what I should pursue with all my heart, soul, mind, body, and strength. Let your Word begin to form in me a new attitude and commitment to good works. Help me to see why doing good should be so basic and prevalent in the lives of all who profess Jesus as Lord and Savior. Amen.

Day 2

Titus 2:11

"For the grace of God has appeared,
bringing salvation to all people"

THE LETTER TO TITUS, though brief, is packed with meaning. This
is seen even in verse 11. Several quick comments are in order.

First, the subject of the verse is "the grace of God." "Grace"
here has two related senses. On the one hand, it refers to God's
benevolence towards mankind: his attitude is one of favor and
help. On the other hand, "grace" also describes the effect of God's
kindness, namely the birth of a kind and loving people. In this
sense, we should understand "the grace of God" as a transformative agent.

Second, Paul specifies that God's "grace" is "saving grace": its
ultimate purpose is to bring "salvation to all people." God is on a
great rescue mission because all are destined to die and suffer his
wrath because of sin. He has resolved to bring salvation through
the death of his Son.

Third, the operative verb is "has appeared." The verb could
also translate as "has been manifested" or "has been spotlighted."
The point is that "the will of God" is not some tantalizing insight
that's only accessible to the holy of holies. In Christ Jesus, God has
made his will abundantly clear—to bring salvation to all people.

In sum, verse 11 teaches that God is bringing salvation to all; and he is inviting us to participate in his mission. You know that you know him when your priorities align with his plan to save.

Prayer

Father in Heaven, you are good. You did not leave humanity to spiral into destruction and death. Instead, you revealed your grace in your Son to express your kindness and favor to those who turn to you. Thank you for revealing your heart to see all people come to faith. Let this clear revelation of your redemptive purpose reshape the way I view my life and priorities. Amen.

Day 3

Titus 2:11

"For the grace of God has appeared,
bringing salvation to *all* people"

THAT THESE WORDS WOULD have come from the mouth of Paul is
striking. Had he said, "For the grace of God has appeared, bringing
salvation to *Israel*," that would have made sense. After all, Paul was
a committed Jew. In Galatians 1:14 he writes, "And I was advancing in Judaism beyond many of my own age among my people, so
extremely zealous was I for the traditions of my fathers." I'm not
sure whether it would be proper to label him with modern terms
like "racist," "elitist," or "ethnocentric." But, prior to his conversion,
he believed in a clear distinction between Jew and Gentile and
sought to maintain such a "dividing wall of hostility" (Ephesians
2:14).

The gospel, however, engendered a new perspective. He began to make radical statements like, "for *all* have sinned and fall
short of the glory of God" (Romans 3:23), and, "There is neither
Jew nor Greek . . . for you are all one in Christ Jesus" (Galatians
3:28). Perhaps most surprising were his new autobiographical
statements: "The saying is trustworthy and deserving of full acceptance, that Christ Jesus came into the world to save sinners,
of whom I am the foremost. But I received mercy for this reason,
that in me, as the foremost, Jesus Christ might display his perfect
patience as an example to those who were to believe in him for

eternal life" (1 Timothy 1:15–16). In light of Christ and the Great Commission to "make disciples of all nations" (Matthew 28:19), Paul understood God's indiscriminate redemptive purposes and thus had to die to his previous way of life.

As we continue to reflect on the pursuit of good works, it may serve us to recall Jesus' words, "And if you greet only your brothers, what more are you doing than others? Do not even the Gentiles do the same?" (Matthew 5:47). Jesus was teaching his disciples to love even their enemies, but the underlying principle is applicable. If we do good works only for those who are like us, whether in terms of race, ethnicity, socio-economic class, then we are no different from the world. But if we resolve to show kindness to "all people," then—like Paul—we evidence a deep understanding of God's grace that is saving "all people." Perhaps a first step in our pursuit of good would be to confess our excluding tendencies.

Prayer

God, your heart is for all nations and your grace for all people. I confess my racism, I repent of my elitism, I own my ethnocentrism. Help me to perceive the subtle ways these tendencies have shaped my life, and grant me conviction and strength to love all without discrimination, for your glory. Amen.

Day 4

Titus 2:12

"*training us,* that by renouncing ungodliness and worldly passions,
we might live in the present age soberly and justly and godly"

THE GRACE OF GOD accomplishes many things. The person who
has been loved much will love much; the person who has been
forgiven will forgive. But today, grace is hardly ever associated
with rigorous training. It's not seen as a catalyst for change, the
first drop leading to countless ripple effects. It's something that
warms my heart and occasionally makes me a kinder person. But
it doesn't lead to any deep and lasting change in my life.

Therefore, it's surprising that Paul uses the term "training" to
describe one of the main purposes or effects of grace. "Training"
translates the Greek term *paideuō*, which can mean:

1. bringing up a child and guiding him toward maturity;

2. morally disciplining an adult;

3. flogging, as a form of legal punishment of a transgressor.[1]

The common denominator of all three definitions is the idea of
tuning a person to a correct standard. A child must learn not to
step on other children in the playground. A husband must learn
not to yell at his wife. A burglar must learn not to steal but to work
so that he has something to give. *Paideuō* means effecting the

1. Friberg, s.v.

7

kind of deep change a new recruit experiences in Marine Corps training. In short, Paul is emphasizing that God's grace cannot be conceived of as anything less than a transformative agent.

I think regularly about how the Christian life should be thought of neither in terms of being radical nor ordinary. The more fitting term seems to be purposeful. A person training to run a marathon knows that every part of her life—her diet, sleeping schedule, social life—must change if she wants to finish the race. An aspiring musician who wants to play at Carnegie Hall knows that he will have to renounce much leisure in order to pursue countless hours of deliberate practice. Similarly, a convert that learns of grace's purpose to create "a people . . . who are zealous for good works" (2:14) should realize that his life cannot remain the same. His life must be characterized by the pursuit of sobriety, justice, and godliness. We will reflect further on what Paul means. For now, it's worthwhile to meditate on the consequential impact that the grace of God should have.

Prayer

Father in Heaven, expand my understanding of grace. Let your grace become a disciplining agent in my life that causes me to be more purposeful about everything. I confess that I cheapen grace to something that assures me of eternal life but demands nothing of my present life. Forgive me and use my disciplined life to bring salvation to the many who have yet to experience your perfect grace in your perfect Son. Amen.

Day 5

Titus 2:12

"training us, that by renouncing ungodliness and worldly passions,
we might live in the present age soberly and justly and godly"

THOUGH OUR MAIN PREOCCUPATION may be with getting into heaven, God is equally concerned with how we live "in the present age." The purpose of grace's *paideuō* is that we might live according to sobriety, justice, and godliness: grace dictates a new way to life, a new pursuit and ambition in life.

The key phrase in verse 12 is "the present *age*." The phrase recalls verse 1:2, which reads, "in hope of *ageless* life, which God . . . promised *ages* ago." Thus, the apostle's audience is invited to adopt a rich—interconnected—perspective on the present life. They are to view it both from the past and toward the future. Ageless life, which will be realized when Christ returns, was promised before the ages began and has been partially revealed in the present with Christ's first appearance. Because of his death and resurrection, all who are united to him by faith are guaranteed eternal life, a present reality that will come to fruition in Christ's second appearance. In sum, Paul summons us to approach "the present age" as those who were known by the Ageless One before the world began and as those who are bound to ageless glory.

Once this immense reality spills into our souls, we better understand why we should pursue sober, just, and godly lives. Strictly speaking, "soberly" means "having a sound or healthy mind," which is possible only when we view life in relation to our past and future. Knowing that we are bound to glory puts all our joys and sorrows in perspective: sorrow is fleeting and joy is teasing. It also helps us to prioritize well. Specifically, we are called to pursue justice—to live "justly." In the new heaven and new earth, the poor will not be silenced, children will not be orphaned, and widows will not be exploited, for God's justice will reign. As present citizens of this coming kingdom, we must seek to reflect this future reality now. Finally, "godly" refers to becoming completed devoted to the One who has known us even before we were born. It means living out of a deep conviction that I am heading toward a splendor beyond my wildest imagination solely because of God's unfailing love.

Prayer

God, thank you for promising me eternal life even before time began. Thank you for accomplishing eternal life through the death and resurrection of your Son. And thank you for guaranteeing that promised life by sending your Spirit. Help me to see my present life in relation to what you did in the past and will do in the future. As I gain perspective, let my life increasingly reflect the marks of sobriety, justice, and godliness. Amen.

Day 6

Titus 2:12

"training us, that by *renouncing ungodliness and worldly passions,*
we might live in the present age soberly and justly and godly"

THE PURSUIT OF SOBER, just, and godly lives in the present age depends on the complementary practices of renouncing our former patterns of life and transforming our vision of the future. Today we reflect on the first—"renouncing ungodliness and worldly passions."

Perhaps the best place to begin is to meditate on the object of renunciation—"ungodliness and worldly passions." "Ungodliness" should not be understood as a synonym for atheism. In this period, there was no such thing. Everyone was professedly religious, regularly seeking to earn the favor of gods through great sacrifices and victories. Paul likely means living as if *the* God of creation and redemption has not revealed himself in Christ Jesus—living as if the life, death, and resurrection of Christ have no real significance on how we think about the present and the future. Consider the person who returns from an uplifting retreat or short-term mission trip. He is deeply moved by the things he has seen and heard. Yet, there isn't any deep or lasting change once he returns to "real" life. Paul summons us to renounce this kind of ungodliness.

"Worldly passions" expresses "natural cravings" or "the desires of your upbringing and culture." For some, the desire is for financial security; for others, luxury. Some crave esteem, others acceptance. "Worldly" refers to earthly standards that do not align with the values of God's kingdom. Unpacking the "worldly passions" that dictate our lives is difficult because they are usually silent and subtle but all-powerful. Though we are a new creation in Christ, it is very difficult to experience full freedom from the cravings that have played such an integral role in our lives.

"Renouncing ungodliness and worldly passions," therefore, is demanding work.[1] Tara Westover, in her New York Times bestseller *Educated*, illustrates this well. She suffered unimaginable abuse for years even into adulthood. Yet, she could not let go of her family. In fact, she refused to do so even though this was the most sensible decision. Becoming estranged from her family seemed more painful (and quite possibly was) than the severe abuse she endured. Similarly, renouncing our old patterns of life is no small endeavor. Apart from the grace Christ gives, abandoning our "old self" is too tall of an order.

But doing so is necessary. It is a dream—a naïve one—to suppose that "you can have it all." For us to pursue philanthropy, we need time, money, resources, focus, and energy. Which means we must be willing to part with so much of our former lives. The apostle could not be clearer: to pursue lives marked by justice, purpose, and grace, we must surrender that which was once normal and even desirable.

Prayer

Lord Jesus, thank you for giving clear guidance on how to pursue the good. I know an integral part of godly living is the complete abandonment of former ways of perceiving and living in the world. Open my eyes to see the subtle but powerful ways that my thinking and desiring do not accord with the standards of your kingdom.

---

1. Jeon, *To Exhort and Reprove*, 79: "The present tense of the participle 'denying' reminds the audience that their present lives must be characterized by a *constant* denial of their former way of existence and its corollary pursuits." Note: In my translation above, I use "renouncing" instead of "denying."

Grant me grace to give up what seems natural and even good so that I might be free to pursue your will. Amen.

Day 7

Titus 2:13

"awaiting the blessed hope, the appearing of
the glory of our great God and Savior Jesus Christ"

THE PURSUIT OF SOBER, just, and godly lives in the present age involves not only renouncing ungodliness and worldly desires but also—and just as much—"awaiting the blessed hope, the appearing of the glory of our great God and Savior Jesus Christ." That is, both our relationship to the past and to the future should drive and shape our present. In fact, it is the very absence of hope that leads to a life mired in monotony and purposelessness.[1]

How are we to think of our "blessed hope"? Paul gives a clue through the repetition of "appearance" language. In verse 11, Paul refers to Christ's first appearance; here, in verse 13, he points to Christ's second appearance. Christ's first appearance serves as a foil for the second. Whereas he was born in weakness, he will appear in power; he was raised in poverty, he will abound in glory; he was made vulnerable, he will be imperishable. In other words, the first and second appearances have in common the same person— "our great God and Savior Jesus Christ." But the natures of their

---

1. See popular memoirs like *The Glass Castle*, *Hillbilly Elegy*, or *Educated* that illustrate this point. In each, the protagonist was able to progress, often in contrast to his or her siblings, because of a different outlook he/she had adopted.

appearances are altogether antithetical. When he returns, the only fitting descriptor for his coming will be "glory."

We long for this second appearance because of our union with Christ.[2] In marriage, the two become one. Therefore, what is true for one is true for the other. If I win the lottery, my spouse rejoices because what is mine is hers. If I am diagnosed with cancer, my loss becomes hers. Union with Christ means that his future glory is also mine. Even as Christ will be exalted so that before him every knee should bow and every tongue confess him as Lord, we too—in a manner that boggles the mind and humbles the spirit—will be made coheirs to reign with him even over the angels. How can those with such a "blessed hope" live without a sense of anticipation!

C. S. Lewis famously wrote, "If you read history you will find that the Christians who did most for the present world were just those who thought most of the next . . . It is since Christians have largely ceased to think of the other world that they have become so ineffective in this."[3] Paul says likewise in these verses. The pursuit of good works in this present life will depend largely on our ability to forgo many of the pleasures and comforts of this life. And the main way to loosen the grips of such comforts and pleasures is by living in anticipation of treasure that "neither moth nor rust destroys" (Matthew 6:20). Therefore, the ability (literally) to abound in philanthropy in the present age depends directly on how we train ourselves and others to fantasize about a future that has Christ as its center.

Prayer

Jesus, our God and Savior, stretch my imagination beyond the confines of early retirement, open golf courses, and picturesque

---

2. Jeon, *To Exhort and Reprove*, 84: "Thus the relative clause highlights for the audience the *substitutionary* nature of Christ's death: he died for their sake. In addition, the pronoun 'us' communicates that the death of Christ is not only *substitutionary but also uniting.*"

3. Lewis, *Mere Christianity*, 134.

beaches. Let me fantasize regularly about that day when all will behold your glory and when all things will be made new; that day when your appearing will defeat death itself, bringing to naught all sorrow, disease, and mourning. Help me to live purposefully in the present in view of the day of glory, which brings so much clarity and focus on what matters in this brief life. Amen.

Day 8

Titus 2:14

"who gave himself for our sake, to free us from all lawlessness and to purify for himself a chosen people who are zealous for good works."

IN VERSE 14, PAUL circles back and identifies Jesus Christ as both the grace that has appeared (2:11) and the foundation of our blessed hope (2:13). In a brief stroke, he summarizes what Christ accomplished for his people and, more so, why he did it.

For a moment, let's consider a very basic question: "Jesus, why did you die for me?" The answer is found here: "I died to free you from the rule of sin and to make you a part of my special people, a people committed to doing good." If ever a person were wrestling with the question of identity and purpose, he or she need look no further than this verse. Previously, outside of our union with Christ, we were captives to lawlessness; but now in Christ we have come under his rule and are called to partake in the marvelous work of reflecting his glory through commendable works.

When I meditate on this verse, the scene of Jesus and Barabbas standing before Pilate and the crowd comes to mind.[1] Though guilty, Barabbas is set free; though innocent, Jesus is condemned. Here we have a vivid illustration of what it meant for Christ to "give himself" in order to free another. The only way we will ever fully give ourselves to the cause of Christ, especially in the form of good works, is when we come to believe that we owe him every-

1. For further reflection, see Jeon, *A New King*, 12–14.

thing. Had he not willingly and graciously laid down his life, even now we would remain under the power of sin. But now we are a new creation. In fact, the term "chosen" literally means "owned as a rich and distinctive possession."[2] Through the blood of Christ we have been purified from the pollution of our former lives and are counted as his prized possession.

And as his prized possession—*not* in order to become it—we have been set apart to be obsessed about doing good. Christ did not die so that we could enjoy every pleasure under the sun. That is, our present lives are not our own to live however we please as we await Jesus' return. We are called to live sober, just, and godly lives, which according to verse 14 is synonymous to living with a zeal "for good works." Why did Christ die on our behalf? So that we might bear much fruit for his glory. To do otherwise is to fail to honor his great sacrifice for us.

Prayer

Jesus, thank you for willingly laying down your life in my place. Your death has ransomed me from the power of sin and has made me your prized possession. Your revealed Word makes clear that my life is not my own, that I am a member of your chosen people and therefore am called to be given over to good works. Drill in me a conviction that philanthropy should shape my existence as an outworking of my new identity in you. Give me a zeal to proclaim your great salvation, especially through a supernatural zeal for good works. Amen.

2. Friberg, s.v.

Day 9

Titus 2:15

"Speak of these things; urge and correct with all authority.
No one should ignore you."

GOOD WORKS—DO THEY REALLY matter? Few would be so in-
clined to reject their necessity, but the belief that they are optional
can sneak in. This is especially the case when one believes that God
"saved us, not because of works that we ourselves did in righteousness, but because of his own mercy" (3:5). Ironically, sometimes
it's the very preaching of the gospel that leads to the mistaken
conclusion that good works are not that important. Paul appears
to be combating such ideas at 2:15 by commanding Titus and all
believers, "No one should ignore you." That is, no one should suppose that all this talk on good works is inconsequential.

Verse 15 is really about culture-making among believers. The
apostle exhorts his audience, "Speak of these things," which is likely a reference to commendable works. Paul wants the topic of our
conversations to go beyond work, kids, vacation, and sports. The
stuff we speak of, after all, eventually forms the culture we breathe.
One pair of researchers noted that they can tell what a church is
all about simply from the Sunday announcements.[1] Paul's point is
that the "things" that should occupy much of our conversation is
our zeal for commendable works (as exemplified in 2:1–10).

---

1. Rainer and Geiger observe: "We have learned that the announcements
given during the worship services can tell a lot about the church. They typically
are a good indication of the priorities of the church" (*Simple Church*, 54).

But Paul goes further. He commands Titus to "urge and correct with all authority." It is as if Paul predicts that Titus will encounter opposition. Sometimes the opposition will be open and fierce. But more often it is quiet and passive; it's the sort that publicly concedes to the importance of good works but fails to take any action. To "urge" means so much more than to suggest. Paul commands Titus to inform the believers under his cares, "You really *must* pursue good works—this isn't optional, this isn't excusable because of busyness." Moreover, for those who persist in fruitless lives, Titus is to "correct." Yes, Paul has the audacity to say that such persons must be convinced of their error and perhaps even rebuked for living out of step with the gospel (2:14). So vital is it that believers, both collectively and individually, engage in good that Paul summons Titus to "urge and correct with all authority" until philanthropy becomes part and parcel of a church's culture.

This verse leaves us with many questions to ponder. In general, do my conversations with other believers gravitate towards how we are pursuing good in our personal lives and in the life of the church? Does my church emphasize the need for good works? Do our leaders regularly "urge and correct with all authority" to help build such a culture? Am I seeking to support various initiatives, or have I adopted the belief that good works are optional and even negligible? It might be helpful to remember that the "authority" Paul has in view is derivative; that is, Paul is summoning Titus to speak with the authority of Christ. Thus, to ignore this exhortation to do good is ultimately to disregard Christ's own lordship.

Prayer

Lord Jesus, may I not neglect this fundamental call to build a culture that is devoted to good works. Forgive me for the many excuses that have led me to believe that such neglect is acceptable in your eyes. Teach me to be more deliberate even in my conversations. Give me a receptive heart to the urging and even rebuking of my leaders. In this way, let my life and my church abound in good so that many would see the Father and give him glory. Amen.

Day 10

Titus 3:1–2

"Remind them to be submissive to rulers and authorities,
to be obedient, to be ready for every good work, to be peaceable and
gentle; in sum, remind them to show consideration toward all people."

IT MAY BE HELPFUL to take a step back and remember what is most
important to Paul. Few things mattered to him more than seeing
all people come to salvation through the gospel. Elsewhere he
writes about becoming all things to all people to win as many as
possible (1 Corinthians 9:22). Even here in the Letter to Titus, he
exhibits much concern to guard the reputation of the gospel (2:5).

But even from the beginning, Christianity was looked upon
with suspicion because it was so different. All other religious
groups made sense because they shared common ancestry or in-
terest. This was not the case for Christians. Moreover, the radical
implications of union with Christ, which removed any distinction
between Jew and Gentile, man and woman, slave and free, would
have appeared disruptive even not treasonous. In short, the road
for sharing the gospel was checkered with profound challenges.

Recognizing such hostility, Paul understood the critical role
that "consideration toward all people" plays in the advance of the
gospel. The commands "to be submissive to rulers and authorities,
to be obedient, to be ready for every good work, to be peaceable
and gentle" are specific applications of the more general call to be
model citizens and philanthropists. If ever believers were going to

gain an audience with the Roman empire, they would have to do so through their piety and goodness. This is why Paul writes a few verses earlier, "Show yourself in all respects to be a model of good works . . . so that an opponent may be put to shame, having nothing evil to say about us" (2:7).

In her stimulating book, *The Gospel Comes with a House Key*, Rosaria Butterfield makes a similar point. She argues that the only way to gain a hearing in a world that has become increasingly hostile toward and suspicious of Christians is to abound in good, especially in the form of hospitality. She defines hospitality as the commitment to love our immediate neighbors, in hope that they might become friends and perhaps even family in Christ Jesus. Her point, which she models so well, echoes what Paul writes in the opening verses of Titus 3—to show consideration and kindness to all people.

Whom do we exclude from "all people"? That is, whom have we—consciously or not—resolved *not* to show courtesy and help? Are we too busy "to be ready for every good work"? Or are we taking steps towards creating "margin time," as Butterfield calls it, so that we can have unhurried conversations and meals with those who have yet to come to faith?[1] In what ways are we needlessly belligerent? Are we participating in what has become the common practice of reviling those in authority? Here again it is worth noting 2:7: "Show yourself in all respects to be a model of good works . . . so that an opponent may be put to shame, having nothing evil to say about us."

Prayer

Jesus, you are the Lord of all people, and you have called me to engage the world as your hands and feet. Remind me to make every effort to be a model citizen and a doer of good; to avoid gratuitous conflicts and to show respect for all. I admit that my piety has been far too individualistic, focusing mainly—if not entirely—on my

---

1. Butterfield, *Gospel Comes with a House Key*, 12

personal walk with you. Like the apostle, give me a passion to see the nations come to faith through my radically ordinary commitment to be present and to abound in good. Amen.

Day 11

Titus 3:3

"For we ourselves were once also senseless,
disobedient, deceived, slaves to various passions and pleasures,
passing our days in evil and envy, despicable, hating one another."

Verse 3 reminds the original audience (and us) of what we were like prior to our union with Christ. Still, it poses some difficulty for the decent secularist. The description—"passing our days in evil and envy, despicable, hating one another"—seems exaggerated. At least, it doesn't seem to be a fair representation of many non-Christians who are in many ways far more admirable than many professing Christians.

To make sense of verse 3, we need to remember that this is a "spiritual" perspective. That is, this is a perspective that a person can have only after the Spirit of Christ has convicted one of sin. Paul, who includes himself among "we ourselves," didn't have such a "low" self-assessment prior to encountering the risen Lord. Philippians 3:3–6, in fact, suggests the opposite: "as to righteousness under the law, blameless." (v. 6). Why, then, does he now say that he too was once "senseless, disobedience, [and] deceived"? This is possible only by "the work of God's Spirit," who "convinces us of our sin and misery, enlightens our minds in the knowledge of Christ, and renews our wills."[1] Since this perspective is the result of a supernatural work, moral secularists can't see themselves in this

1. *Westminster Shorter Catechism* 31.

way. Seeing oneself as a "slave to various passions and pleasures" and therefore guilty before the one true King is nothing less than a miracle.[2]

But, again, how does remembering our depravity relate to being ready for every good work and showing kindness to all? Remembering our own lostness makes a world of a difference because it fills us with compassion and hope. Christians are both the most cynical and the most optimistic people in the world. On the one hand, we don't believe that people are inherently good. We don't believe that the main problem in this world is ignorance, as if human beings would do the right thing if they just knew better. We believe that the main problem with the world is our brokenness and rebellion. Though we know God exists and cannot escape his imprint on us, we continue to try to suppress that knowledge and live as if we were our own masters.[3] We are inescapably worshipers who continue to exalt created realities—especially the self—above God. We know that there is something profoundly wrong within us, and yet we hate those who see beyond our disguises. None could be more cynical than the Christian.

Yet, Christians are filled with hope. If "once" we were lost but are now found, could not others—who are not different from what "we ourselves were once"—also be changed by mercy? The only reason we wouldn't believe this is if we secretly believed that we were immanently made of better stuff. But if we identify with those who are outside of Christ, as Paul does so here, we believe that God can also save and transform them, especially through our commitment to do good. Thus, remembering that "we ourselves were once" lost is critical to nurturing a life committed to philanthropy.

2. For a brief but insightful treatment on idolatry, see Keller, *Counterfeit Gods*, xiv.

3. Jeon, *To Exhort and Reprove*, 94: "The participle 'enslaved' . . . reiterates to the audience one of the apostle's core convictions: everyone is 'enslaved' to someone or something . . . Redemption through 'Jesus Christ,' then, is not a shift from enslavement to freedom but a transference from one rule to another. Specifically, it is a transference from being 'enslaved to various desires and pleasures' to being 'enslaved' to God as a 'special people, zealous for commendable works' (2:14)."

Prayer

God, may I remember that I too was once "senseless, disobedient, deceived, a slave to various passions and pleasures, passing my days in evil and envy, despicable, hating one another." And by remembering, may I be filled with compassion and hope. Surely if you were able to save even this chief of sinners, you can do the same for others. Therefore, I pursue kindness to all, believing that even those who appear hopeless are not outside of your saving power. Amen.

Day 12

Titus 3:4–5a

"But when the graciousness and philanthropy of God our Savior appeared, he saved us, not because of works that we ourselves did in righteousness, but because of his own mercy"

THE NEXT UNIT OF Titus 3 (verses 4–7) is so dense that it makes sense for us to break it down into separate reflections. Over the next four devotions, we'll consider how the passage reflects on *what* God did, *when*, *how*, and *why*. All this we'll connect back to our broader concern, namely that God's people are called to pursue good works. In today's reflection we focus on the *what*: God "saved us, not because of works that we ourselves did in righteousness, but because of his own mercy."

First, we should recall how verse 3:3 concludes. Paul says that we were despicable; we lived without any awareness of the significance of Christ's life, death, and resurrection. The fitting response to such ignorance, rebellion, and evil would have been divine condemnation. Verses 4–7, however, says that God responded in an altogether different and extraordinary way. We acted in malice, "*but*" God responded in mercy.

The heart of verses 4–7 is the declaration, "But . . . God saved us." Though we were once enslaved to lawlessness (2:14) and worldly desires (3:3), God redeemed us by sending his Son. And, to avoid any misunderstanding, Paul makes clear through a blatant contrast that God's salvation came as a gift, not as a reward. God saved us "not because of" any good works that we performed as an expression of an inherent righteousness. Rather, he saved us according to "his own mercy." Our salvation has nothing to do with us—we did nothing to earn it. God saved us because he is compassionate toward sinners, giving them what they do not deserve because he is kind.

None, then, can boast. None can relish in his or her moral achievement, nor can one wallow in his or her failures. Everything I am today is solely by the sovereign mercy of God.

If all this is true, and we believe that it is, then what must be said of any follower of Christ? As we engage a world that was once familiar to us, what main impression should we make on all we encounter? Titus 3:4–7 suggests that grace should be our trademark. We don't stick it to people even though that's what they may deserve. We don't show kindness on the basis of their moral performance. In other words, we don't act according to our natural selves that were driven by envy and hatred. Instead, we extend to all a kindness that is supernatural because it stems from our own experience of divine grace. If ever a person were to ask, "Why are you so good to me?" our answer should be, "Because the Lord has first shown me mercy and has called me to do likewise."

Prayer

God, thank you for saving me. All that I am and all that I have, both now and in the future, are because of your sovereign mercy. I deserved rejection, but you chose not to relate to me according to my merits but according to your mercy. Grant me now power to extend kindness to the loathsome and hateful, to those who do not deserve my kindness. As you have tangibly loved me through your Son, may I abound in concrete good for my enemies, for your glory. Amen.

Day 13

Titus 3:4–5a

"But when the graciousness and philanthropy of God our Savior appeared, he saved us, not because of works that we ourselves did in righteousness, but because of his own mercy"

HAVING CONSIDERED WHAT GOD has done for us, we now reflect on *when* God saved us. Verse 4 ("But *when* the graciousness and philanthropy of God our Savior appeared") is to be heard in contrast to the adverb "once" in verse 3 ("But we ourselves were once also senseless . . .). This is not a pedantic observation. Paul means to highlight the decisive change that has taken place in history. The way we apply it personally is through the use of "formerly-but-now" language. Formerly ("once") we acted ignorantly; but now ("when") that God has revealed his gospel, we can no longer live in our former days of evil and hatred.

There is an obvious echo in 3:4 of 2:11 ("For the grace of God has appeared, bringing salvation to all people"). But why the shift in subject from "grace" to "graciousness and philanthropy"? What nuance is Paul trying to bring out? This first term "graciousness" occurs regularly in the Psalms to describe God's kindness, particularly as it is expressed in concrete help toward his people (e.g., Psalm 24:7; 67:11; 84:13). The second term "philanthropy," which literally means "love-of-people," is found in Greco-Roman literature to express hospitality—a "love-of-strangers" expressed tangibly in food, drink, and shelter. Both terms would have been familiar to the original recipients of the letter as a descriptor for benefactors and ideal rulers.[1] Perhaps the nuance in 3:4, which is only implicit in 2:11–14, is this: the former passage focuses on the purpose of Christ's self-giving, namely that we might become a people zealous for good works. Verse 3:4 focuses on God being the original Philanthropist. The connection is that as much as God has called us to do good to all people, he has first done so by saving us.

Earlier in the letter, Paul describes elders as those who are known for being *philoxenon* ("lovers-of-strangers") and *philagathon* ("lovers-of-good"; 1:8). The connection could not be clearer. If God reveals himself as the paradigmatic Philanthropist whose philanthropy is manifested in salvation, and if a person has experienced such graciousness, then the inevitable fruit must be love-of-strangers and love-of-good toward all people. In sum, it is the revelation of the gospel that moves us from what we "once" were—slaves to hedonism—to what we now are—a people zealous for good. God's grace cannot be ineffectual.

Have God's "graciousness and philanthropy" interrupted and changed the direction of your life? God calls us to be model citizens, to be ready to engage in good, to show kindness to all because his kindness has invaded our former lives and given us a radically new framework. Of the false teachers earlier in the letter, Paul makes this scathing remark: "God they profess to know, but by their works they deny" (1:16). Their profession of faith is worthless because their lives lack the divine philanthropy God has revealed in salvation. How are we faring?

Prayer

Savior, I too was once senseless, a slave to pleasure and full of hatred. You responded by sending your Son to die in my place. In doing so, you showed yourself as the ultimate Philanthropist. The teaching is clear. Now, having received such graciousness and philanthropy, love-of-stranger and love-of-good should mark my life. Show me how I must turn from my former life to a new life characterized by a readiness to do good. Amen.

1. Jeon, *To Exhort and Reprove*, 103.

Day 14

Titus 3:5b–6

"by the washing of regeneration and renewal done by the Holy Spirit,
whom he poured out on us richly through Jesus Christ our Savior"

HAVING CONSIDERED THE WHAT and *when* of our salvation, we
now turn to the *how*: "by the washing of regeneration and renewal
done by the Holy Spirit, whom he poured out on us richly through
Jesus Christ our Savior" (3:5b–6). This is a mouthful. Helpful for
understanding is the classic Cinderella story.

Suppose you have a fairly young woman. She comes from
what most would consider a dysfunctional home. She was once
married, is currently barely employable, and has signs of various
addictions. But out of nowhere a charming and successful man,
who leads a company that is committed to profit and philanthropy,
pursues her. In the process, she becomes a new person. She is
removed from abusive settings; she receives counseling; she has
a picturesque wedding; and she now enjoys all the privileges of
being the wife of this successful entrepreneur and philanthropist.
The only expectation her husband has is for her to join him in
building a better society.

This kind of story is rare, found mainly in the annals of Dis-
ney. But every story is a faint echo of the one true gospel story.
And here in this verse-and-a-half, Paul makes three points, all of
which highlight our new status as those who are set apart for good
works. First, he reminds us that the Holy Spirit has made us clean.

Scholars debate the precise meaning of the convoluted phrase "the washing of regeneration and renewal done by the Holy Spirit." But this much can be agreed, that an inner spiritual cleansing has happened. We have been purified in preparation for our marriage to Christ.

Second, the language of God's rich outpouring of the Holy Spirit echoes Joel 2:8, which prophesied such a day. Thus, the outpouring of the Spirit signifies a decisive shift in history: believers now live in the age of fulfillment. Third, this unique and extraordinary blessing has come about through their marriage to Christ ("through Jesus Christ our Savior"). Paul has already made clear that God's gift of salvation is not in response to any merit on our part but according to his own mercy. In like fashion, God's gift of the Holy Spirit comes only through Christ: we receive every good blessing because we are in him.

Who are we? We are God's chosen people who have been made clean by his Spirit: God has removed all our filthy rags. We are a people who live in a unique time in the history of salvation as recipients of God's Spirit. Hence, we are uniquely empowered. Finally, we are a people united to Jesus Christ, the great Savior who will someday make all things new. If all this is true, it's a wonder if we're giving ourselves to anything other than abounding in good for the glory of the One who has saved us.

Prayer

Savior and Lord, I confess that I still live according to the former patterns of my life. I live as if I have not been washed, as if I still abide in the age of death and darkness, as if I am not known and loved by you. But the gospel declares otherwise: I am clean, I am a participant of the age of the Holy Spirit, and I am one with Christ. As such, let me live with freedom from guilt, ignorance, and loneliness. Fill me with passion to participate in the great work of redemption. Amen.

Day 15

Titus 3:7

"so that being justified by his grace we might become heirs
according to the hope of eternal life."

HAVING CONSIDERED THE *WHAT*, *when*, and *how* of our salvation,
we now turn to the last part of this section, which deals with the
why. To what end did God save us? Verse 7 answers: "so that being
justified by his grace we might become heirs according to the hope
of eternal life." Let's again consider a story.

Kara, only ten years old, was told by Chad and Kate, her foster parents, that they had something to share with her later that
evening. As she reclined in bed, she wondered, "Are they going
to tell me it's time to move on to my next 'family'? Why does this
always happen around the holiday season?" This was Kara's third
foster home. Although she had always been on her best behavior,
one family after another gave her up, often saying, "This was never
meant to be permanent." Her heart raced as she heard Chad and
Kate make their way up the stairs.

Chad asked her to come out of bed. They met at the door
post, he knelt down and placed his rough hands softly on her
shoulder. Kate watched with one hand covering her mouth, the
other hand drooping as if confused. He then gently said, "Kara,
you're ours now. We got all the paperwork done. You're officially
part of our family. Merry Christmas, our precious daughter." As
her eyes welled up with tears, Chad then added, "This had always
been the plan. We just wanted to make sure everything was lined

up before telling you." As she began to convulse with elation, Kate swooped in, and the three held one another, weeping away years of sadness.

Later that night, Kara was still shaking in her bed. She relived the conversation again and again. She could hardly grasp her new reality. No longer was she an orphan. No longer would she live in a state of fear, wondering when she would be transferred to another home. She marveled at the words of the man who was now her father, that she was officially part of the family. Most of all, she couldn't believe that this had always been the plan. Unbeknownst to her, her foster parents had been plotting all along to make her a part of their family.

The conclusion of Titus 3:4–7 reminds me of Kara's story. The mention of "being justified" highlights how we have been trans-ferred from one sphere of envy and hatred to another sphere of righteousness. Moreover, our new identity is not just forensic and legal but also deeply personal. As "heirs," we are full members of God's family, destined to reign with Christ for all eternity. Finally, the language "*according* to the hope of eternal life" means that all this was always God's plan, made "before the ages began" (1:3). In other words, before we could do anything good or bad, God chose to save us in Christ.

Like Kara, we should be filled with wonder and awe. God saved us in order to make us part of his family and recipients of glory. Perhaps the only fitting word that captures the underlying dynamic is "grace": we get what we don't deserve because God is kind. And as those now destined to receive eternal life, God calls us to extend the same kind of compassion and philanthropy we have received in salvation. In light of 3:7, verses 3:1–3 read very differently for a person that comes to grips with how much grace he has received.

Prayer

Almighty God, I praise you for saving me, for declaring me righ-teous, for making me a coheir of glory, and for knowing me before the foundations of the world. It's all by your grace. Help me now to live in a manner worthy of the gospel. Empower me to extend to all people the grace you have shown me, including those I would otherwise envy and hate. Amen.

Day 16

Titus 3:8

"Faithful is the word; and of these things I want you to assert,
so that those who have believed in God may
be intentional about dedicating themselves to good works.
These things are excellent and profitable for people."

CHRISTIANITY IS GOOD FOR the world. At least it should be. Alas, so much of our history, ranging from the Crusades to financial and abuse scandals, has suggested otherwise. And sometimes our failures do not have to be as egregious as murder in the name of Christ. Sometimes they can be as basic as being bad neighbors—present in a given locale but otherwise absent other than on Sundays. At best, in this case we are a force neither for good nor for evil; we just are, which is unfortunate and foreign to the testimony of Scripture.

Verse 8 follows a basic movement. It begins with the assertion "Faithful is the word." The "word" is likely referring to verses 4–7: we can and must believe that God has saved us by sending his Son and pouring out the Holy Spirit.[1] By grace we are now heirs of glory according to a plan set before the foundations of the world. Verse 8 continues with the exhortation that Titus and all proclaimers of the gospel should never tire to reiterate this wonderful news of grace. Yes, we were once mired in envy and hatred, but because of God's great love for us we have been transferred into the domain

1. Though it is possible that Paul also has in view the exhortations in 3:1–2; see Jeon, *To Exhort and Reprove*, 110.

36

of righteousness and are partakers of his work of redemption. The purpose of such reiteration is that those who have professed faith would live purposeful lives, giving themselves over to good works. The fruit of all this is a people whose presence and philanthropy lead to a better society for all.

Tim Keller, founding pastor of Redeemer and bestselling author of *The Reason for God*, regularly said to the members of his church: "We want to become a community that is for the city, so much so that even those who do not believe what we believe will still say, 'We are so glad Redeemer is part of New York City.'" This vision aligns well with what Paul writes: the key marker of a robust orthodoxy is a flourishing society rooted in gospel-driven good works.

Put differently, verse 8 represents a sequence of basic propositions:

1. the more you grasp the gospel through faithful preaching and teaching, the more you understand your identity;
2. the more you understand your identity, the clearer your calling to good works becomes;
3. the clearer your calling becomes, the more you should give yourself over to good works;
4. the more you give yourself to good works for all, the more society flourishes.

Thus, we are left with these probing questions: Has the gospel of grace taken hold of your life? Has it transformed the way you see yourself and your calling? Does intentionality mark your existence? In what ways do you strategize in order to abound in good? Is your neighborhood, school, workplace, church, and general community a better place because of you and your church?

Prayer

God our Savior, the gospel is good news, so good that I sometimes struggle to believe it. This is why I need to hear and meditate on it regularly. May I never lose the wonder of the cross! As the Holy Spirit opens my eyes to behold my new identity in Christ, reorder my loves and my life so that I might fully give myself to doing good. Let my presence and zeal to bless all make clear that Christianity is good for the world. Amen.

Day 17

Titus 3:8

"Faithful is the word; and of these things I want you to assert, so that *those who have believed in God may be intentional about dedicating themselves to good works.*
These things are excellent and profitable for people."

VERSE 8 IS SUCH a rich verse that it's worth meditating on further, specifically the words, "those who have believed in God may be intentional about dedicating themselves to good works." These words echo the main message of the letter, namely that genuine faith is proven by godliness (1:1).[1] They divide into two related parts—a profession of faith and a manifestation of faith.

What does it mean to believe in God? In this letter, it means believing that Christ has come and will come again. It means believing that God predestined to save and adopt us according to his eternal plans. But in the immediate context it means believing that God is *the* ultimate Philanthropist who has graced a loveless world with his beloved Son. Believing in this God means believing that he desires to bless all with his goodness, especially through his chosen people. Believing is not just a matter of individual salvation, though it is not less than that. Believing in God means believing that philanthropy is fundamental to our existence because we have experienced philanthropy from God the Father, God the Son, and God the Holy Spirit (3:4–7).

1. For further reflection, see Jeon, *True Faith.*

The Bible has no place for empty belief. In his memoir *Shoe Dog*, Nike's co-founder, former chairman, and CEO Phil Knight recounts the early days of wanting to do something that aligned with his passion for running; of wanting to build something that would not just outlast his own life but would also make the world a better place for all. Many of Knight's peers were pursuing lucrative and predictable jobs in accounting and finance. Knight, however, chose an unconventional path by establishing a company devoted to making better shoes for all. Knight suffered no shortage of naysayers. Even his father initially doubted the wisdom of Knight's decision to pursue this entrepreneurial path. But, as Knight recalls, his mother believed in him. She had faith that her son had the grit and ability to make his dream a reality. And so she purchased some shoes to express the sincerity of her faith. Such is the kind of faith the Bible requires.

Specifically, what does God expect from his people who have professed faith? He expects them to be intentional. Intentional about budgeting time and money to do good. Intentional about creating "SMART" goals—specific measurable, achievable, relevant, and time-bound ways to help others. Intentional about living modestly in order to be generous. Faith-driven good works will not happen spontaneously. They will require tremendous intentionality—strategic decisions, we might say—to ensure our lives are bearing fruit for the glory of God. The language in verse 8 could not be clearer and more challenging: those who have confessed Jesus as Lord must be purposeful about pursuing a life that is given over to philanthropy. In this regard, well-known philanthropists like Phil Knight, Bill Gates, and Warren Buffet are worthy models to imitate.

Prayer

God, has it not become too easy for me to claim that I believe while failing to pursue a purposeful life marked by good works? Thank you for giving this concrete portrait of genuine faith: to believe in you, the great Philanthropist, is to aspire to become like you.

Convict me to believe that good works matter, not because they merit salvation but because they demonstrate genuine faith. Grant me wisdom and surround me with the right community so that I might learn how to pursue a more purposeful life dedicated to doing good. Amen.

Day 18

Titus 3:9

"But shun moronic debates, genealogies, disputes, and conflicts
about the law; for they are unprofitable and empty."

VERSE 8 MADE CLEAR that the pursuit of a life marked by good
works requires much intentionality, that is, philanthropy is
planned, not the fruit of spontaneity. Verses 9–11 continue this
theme of being purposeful by inviting believers to pay attention
to their interests and to be mindful about their company. Today
we focus on verse 9, an exhortation to "shun . . . unprofitable and
empty" talk.

A basic ingredient to doing good is time. But time is a luxury,
and for many as life progresses, time becomes a scarcer resource.
Given this, Paul beckons believers to master the art of tuning out
what is unhelpful. For the original audience, that meant avoiding
"moronic debates," which usually led to "disputes" and "conflicts"
about things of secondary importance. Moreover, as most know,
almost all debates veer from the subject themselves and devolve
into a clash of egos. Finally, they suck up precious time and energy,
which could otherwise be devoted to more fruitful endeavors.

For us today, engagement in theological debates seems as
likely as encountering a kangaroo with nunchucks. Nevertheless,
the underlying principle remains applicable. Consider how social
media and online forums have led to a deluge of "moronic debates . . . disputes, and conflicts." Recall how much these enraged

you and sucked you dry of your emotional energy and time. And consider what the net effect of such engagement was: the inability to give yourself to profitable good works. In our society that suffers no shortage of ego, discussion, and frivolous information, Paul's exhortation could not be more apt.

The discipline of shunning will look different for each person. For some, it'll involve avoiding office gossip during coffee breaks. For others, it'll involve the difficult decision of reducing time on social media. For others, it'll require checking the ego that feels the need to participate in—and win—every debate. Whatever shunning might look like for you, take inventory of your life. Everyone could afford to scale back from what is "unprofitable and empty" in order to pursue that which is lasting and helpful.

Prayer

God, grant me discipline to live a more purposeful life, especially in the areas that seem benign or insignificant. I fail to recognize how much of my time and energy are expended on debates and issues that are "unprofitable and empty." Enable me to discern what I should shun so that I might steward this short life well in service to all for your glory. Amen.

Day 19

Titus 3:10–11

"Disregard the factious person after a first and second warning, since you know that this sort of person is warped and persists in sin, being self-condemned."[1]

BEFORE REFLECTING ON 3:10–11, we should recall the main purpose of the letter—to promote a life of philanthropy among those who have confessed Jesus as Lord. Paul knows that in order to do so, much more is needed than inspiration. There must be deliberation, a purposefulness in all of life. This includes being especially judicious about our regular company. Of course, this raises a thorny question. Didn't Jesus devote much time to "sinners"? If we don't spend significant time with those who do not believe, how will we ever form deep and authentic relationships with skeptics?

The answer resides in understanding what Paul meant by "disregard" and what type of person he had in mind. First, a few verses earlier, Paul made clear that believers ought to show respect for all. Somehow, then, we must "disregard" a person in an artful manner, observing this complementary command to be courteous to all. Second, the command doesn't mean that we should disregard her inherent glory as an image-bearer. That is, we are always

1. The command given in 3:10–11 requires caution and precision. Some can take it to mean that believers should completely shun "bad" people. A detailed understanding of the different terms and the syntax will help avoid this pitfall; see Jeon, *To Exhort and Reprove*, 114–15.

to treat all people as creatures that have been fearfully and wonderfully made. Rather, the command to "disregard" the troublemaker is a call to break Christian fellowship: don't relate to the person as if she belongs to God's household. Don't view them as a follower of Christ irrespective of what she professes. This doesn't mean that we should cease to love, care, and pray for this person. It simply means that we should have right expectations from such an individual.

So who is this "factious person"? He is the person that has resolved to remain in rebellion. Even the term "factious" carries the nuance of breaking from orthodox teaching. This person has been warned on more than one occasion to cease from promoting heresy and divisive behavior. Still, he persists in sin. Indeed, his resolve to disregard legitimate authority and to be wise in his own eyes has led to a warped outlook on and approach to life. In the end, his demise is his own doing, stemming from a refusal to repent; thus, he is "self-condemned."

Do such people exist? Unfortunately, the answer is an emphatic yes. (Perhaps these verses might be describing you.) The church suffers no shortage of professing believers who have a complete disregard for leadership. They have resolved to continue the pattern of their lives despite the pleas and warnings of other believers. Such persons not only cause division but often require an undue amount of time and energy—resources that could (and should) be devoted to good works. Though this is a difficult command, it's one worth considering. Sometimes, it becomes necessary to part ways with a warped sinner—after repeated and earnest efforts—in order to fulfill our call to devote ourselves to good works. We should never rejoice in broken fellowship. Still, we must not be oblivious to its occasional necessity.

Prayer

God, grant me wisdom to know when it is time to part ways with a professing believer that persists in sin. Help me to first do the difficult work of urging the person toward proper submission to the shepherds and to sincere repentance. Let there always be an air of compassion toward those who have resolved to be "self-condemned." But if the occasion arises, grant me faith to move on so that your summons to do good might not be neglected. Amen.

Day 20

Titus 3:12

"When I send Artemas or Tychicus to you, do your best to come to
me at Nicopolis, for I have resolved to spend the winter there."

WHAT COMES TO MIND when you imagine your retirement? For
more than a few, picturesque beaches and perfect daily weather
fill their imagination. Deadlines are a thing of the past. No longer
is there any need to deal with unreasonable bosses, difficult colleagues, and even more difficult family members. Retirement is
marked by peace, quietness, and comfort.

But every now and then you meet a person who thinks differently about retirement. My father, who in many respects is a son of
Adam, taught me to adopt a different outlook on our final season
of life. Regularly he would say, "All of life must be stewarded unto
the Lord—including your years of retirement." My father retired
early from his lucrative dental practice to serve as an international
missionary. While many of his colleagues have retired and enjoy
traveling between their various homes, my father lives in a foreign
land among people whose culture is alien to his sensibilities. His
accommodations might pass for a two-star hotel in the United
States. Crime and danger are a regular part of his life. But he is
content, knowing that he is not wasting life.

In verse 12, the apostle includes a seemingly insignificant
detail about his plans: "I have resolved to spend the winter [at

Nicopolis]." Nicopolis suffered harsh winters.[1] It was not the sort of place one would rush to for vacation. One can think of it as the opposite of Napa Valley or Hawaii. Still, comfort and convenience never dictated Paul's decisions. Instead, what mattered most was engagement in fruitful labor for the gospel; hence, the decision to go where he was most needed. "Apparently the city was an ideal location for further ministry."[2]

The Letter to Titus is considered one of Paul's last letters. But even during this final season of life and ministry, he gave himself fully to doing good. His example reminds us that all of life falls under the umbrella of stewardship. To be sure, as we age we must slow down and accept the unfortunate but inevitable consequence of the fall. Nevertheless, we must also aspire to bear fruit with the resources, opportunities, and abilities God has allotted in every season. Paul encourages all who profess faith in Christ to dream a greater dream than the American Dream of early and comfortable retirement. Because Christ has come and will come again, believers should pursue the good as they anticipate Christ's return.

Prayer

Lord, your summons to abound in good should permeate all of life. From beginning to end, may I bear fruit for the sake of your gospel and your glory. Help me to fight my natural tendencies to idolize comfort. Enable me to swim against the currents of ease and luxury. Fix my eyes on that day of reckoning when I will give an account for my life. On that day, may it not be said, "I wasted my life." Amen.

---

1. Towner, *Letters*, 801.
2. Jeon, *To Exhort and Reprove*, 117; see also Witherington, *Letters*, 165.

Day 21

Titus 3:13

"Do your best to send forth Zenas the lawyer and Apollos,
making sure they lack nothing."

WHERE DO YOU BEGIN with philanthropy? While the answer to this question is straightforward, visions of grandeur and glory have complicated it. We hear of billionaires like Bill Gates and Warren Buffett who have given enormous sums away to fight disease, poverty, and injustice. We also hear of more grassroot efforts spearheaded by individuals who overcame suffering and tragedy to help others in similar situations. Some of us, though moved by such examples, conclude, "I can never accomplish something so great," and so we set aside the summons to do good.

Verse 13 comes as a timely encouragement. With all of Paul's lofty theological statements about God's great salvation in Christ Jesus, we might expect Paul to challenge believers to now go and change the world. But his exhortation to Titus and the believers with him is surprisingly (perhaps disappointingly) ordinary. He urges them to furnish "Zenas the lawyer and Apollos" with everything they need as the two prepare to leave.[1]

---

1. Jeon, *To Exhort and Reprove*, 117: "'Zenas' is not mentioned anywhere else in the NT. For 'Apollos' (assuming he is the same person associated with Paul in the Corinth-Ephesus mission) see Acts 18:24; 19:1; 1 Cor 1:12; 3:4, 5, 6, 22; 4:6; 16:12."

These two individuals were likely Paul's colleagues who had spent a season ministering to the believers in Crete. In other words, they weren't strangers but well-known individuals. Paul is teaching that when it comes to pursuing good works, the best place to start is with those immediately around you, both in your church and in your neighborhood.[2] Don't be fooled by the happy smiles at church. There is never a shortage of broken marriages, lonely singles, and confused and embittered people in your congregation. Similarly, the needs of your neighbor might become obvious once you take a moment to look. I think of my elderly neighbors who struggle to take out their garbage. I'll probably never find the cure for malaria, but perhaps what God wants is my taking an extra five minutes each week to remove my neighbor's garbage.

God's providence, which refers to his rule over all things, frees us from drowning in the existential waves of having to figure out God's great plan for our lives. The call to abound in good begins with the ordinary, with tangibly meeting the needs of those God has placed in our lives to serve and bless.

Prayer

Sovereign God, you alone can rescue, you also can save a world that doesn't want to be saved. Thank you that the burden of renewing all things rests with you alone. You call me to something far more ordinary—but still significant, namely doing good for the people in my life here and now. At least let that be a place for me to begin as I take my first steps toward a philanthropic life. Help me to think outside of myself in order to see and meet the needs around me. Amen.

---

2. I cited earlier Rosaria Butterfield's tremendous book on hospitality, *The Gospel Comes with a House Key*. This book is one of the most moving and yet practical treatments on the topic of being a good neighbor.

Day 22

Titus 3:14

"Indeed, our people must learn to devote themselves to
commendable works—*to urgent needs,*
in order not to be unfruitful."

FOR ABOUT A DECADE, I conducted marriage counseling as a
single. When I got married and began to experience the joys
and challenges of married life, my counseling didn't change. The
general wisdom of enduring with grace, listening well, and speaking gently remained the same. At the same time, there was a new
sense of insight and weight: I learned what all these things meant
through practice (and failure!).

This is the sort of learning Paul has in mind in his assertion,
"Indeed, our people must *learn* to devote themselves to commendable works—to urgent needs." Disciples of Christ know that they
should pursue good works. But there is a very real sense that they
don't know how basic this is to their existence and calling until they
start meeting the "urgent needs" of those around them. I would go
so far to say that the "Aha" moment of "This is what it means to fol-
low Christ" doesn't happen until all of our learning has moved us
to action. There is no place for mere theory among believers; "our
people *must* learn to devote themselves to commendable works."

Paul intentionally uses divisive language. "Our people" are to
be distinguished from the false teachers and troublemakers who
make great professions of faith but fail to do any tangible good.

Such people are marked by abstraction, while "our people" are marked by action, action rooted in theological conviction that God is making for himself a people zealous for good works. In this letter, Paul makes clear that what distinguishes the people of God is not just sound theology but also fruitful living: "Our people" get the gospel because they have received sound instruction and because they have learned godliness by doing good.

Anyone who has come to faith experiences this common phenomenon: so much of the Christian life is unlearning old patterns of thinking and living and learning new ones. Hence, Paul regularly uses the language of putting off and putting on (e.g., Ephesians 4:22, 24). If you want to grow in your understanding of what it means to be a member of God's people, Paul says you must learn—via experience—to devote yourself to philanthropy.

Prayer

Loving Master, too often I fall prey to the mistake of confusing knowledge acquisition with spiritual growth. Far too often my knowledge of the gospel and your will outweigh my obedience to do good. By your Spirit, move me from complacent abstraction to concrete philanthropy. May I grasp who I truly am as I engage in a life of good works. Let my life be marked by a deep devotion to meeting the urgent needs around me. Amen.

Day 23

Titus 3:14

"Indeed, our people must learn to devote themselves to
commendable works—to urgent needs,
in order not to be unfruitful."

VERSE 14 ENDS ON a sobering note, that followers of Christ should
"not be unfruitful." Why does Paul use negative language? Why
didn't he say, "in order that they would be fruitful"? From the
perspective of this letter, the reason seems intentional: he means
to call to mind the false teachers whose lives embody fruitless living.[1] Thus, what Paul intends to say here is, "so that our people
would not be like the false teachers" who have demonstrated that
they "are detestable, disobedient, unfit for any good work" (1:16).

But let's reflect for a moment what Paul's pastoral concern
has been. He wants believers to realize the purpose for which they
were saved. Verse 2:14 declared that Christ "gave himself for our
sake . . . to purify for himself a chosen people who are *zealous for
good works.*" We are to dream of doing good, of providing a family
for orphans, sustenance for the hungry, shelter and clothing for

---

1. Jeon, *To Exhort and Reprove*, 119: "Instead of building up the churches
they are 'upsetting whole households, teaching what is not necessary' (1:1).
Instead of 'holding fast to the faithful word' (1:9) they are focusing the 'elect'
(1:1a) on 'Jewish myths and regulations of human beings' (1:14). Instead of
'demonstrating all gentleness to all human beings' (3:2) they are causing the
'word of God' (2:5) to be blasphemed."

the homeless, justice for the oppressed, and healing for the sick. In short, a vision of philanthropy rooted in God's own loving kindness to all mankind must capture our imagination. The Christian life, then, is not about waiting idly as we anticipate our future glory. The Christian life is about laboring with all our might to produce a harvest unto the Lord. Paul has repeatedly described this sort of life with the phrase "good works."

I pastor in an affluent and privileged area. Sadly, what has captured the imagination of so many Christians are upgraded homes, safe neighborhoods, luxurious vacations, fancy clothes, and comfortable retirement. What seems lost is a preoccupation with doing good as an outworking of our membership among the people of God. I'm not suggesting that we can't enjoy God's creation; asceticism and Christianity are not the same thing. Still, it's noteworthy that so few believers are fully given over to philanthropy: we lack Christians who rival the likes of Bill Gates and Warren Buffett in philanthropic zeal. Paul's burden in this letter has been to summon believers to authentic faith, which includes a devotion to philanthropy, "so that [others] may see your good works and give glory to your Father who is in heaven" (Matthew 5:16).

By the power of the Holy Spirit and the encouragement and inspiration of the saints, let us resolve to pursue good works "in order not to be unfruitful."

Prayer

God, Maker and Redeemer, you saved me not according to my good works but unto good works. You saved me by sending Christ and pouring out your Spirit so that I might be passionate about doing good toward all. Let a vision for philanthropy for your glory take root in my imagination and supplant the things I once held so dear. Convict me to believe that you do not want me to be unfruitful. Open my eyes and extend my hands, so that I might meet the immediate and urgent needs around me. Amen.

Day 24

Titus 3:15

"All who are with me greet you.
Greet those who love us in the faith.
Grace be with you all."

VERSE 15 CONCLUDES THIS rich letter with an exchange of greetings and a blessing. In one sense, the exchange of greetings is straightforward. Paul sends greetings on behalf of "all who are with me." Then he commands Titus to greet "those who love us in the faith." But this specification of only "those who love us in the faith" suggests that something more is going on than a simple exchange.

As Paul has done already in this letter, it seems like he is drawing clear lines between those who are "in faith" and outside of faith. These lines are not just along the lines of orthodoxy. True faith in this letter has been defined mainly in terms of a dynamic orthodoxy that comprises sound theology and good works. If this is the case, the greetings sound more like "All who align with my vision of the Christian life, who not only profess godliness but also pursue it through good works—such persons who are my kin 'in faith' send you greetings. Similarly, greet those who love us, that is, those who aspire to hold to sound doctrine and abound in philanthropy in contrast to those who profess faith in God but deny him by their works."

Such apparent exclusivity smells odious to many. Already we live in such a fractured world. What good will come from drawing even more lines between professing believers? This concern is understandable, but it falls short at least in one significant area. For Paul, true faith was a matter of heaven and hell. There are many things we can be wrong about in life. "Perhaps I should have chosen this major instead of that one, or this job instead of that one." But none of this has eternal consequences. This, however, does not hold true with respect to faith. How many will stand before Jesus expecting to hear, "Well done, good and faithful servant," but will be aghast when the words, "I never knew you," fall on their ears! Paul's purpose was never to be unduly discriminatory. Rather, he wanted believers to be confident about their faith; he simply had no place for counterfeit faith.

Are you with the apostle Paul? Do you zealously pursue good works in view of what God has done in Christ and what he will do? Do you live in anticipation of that day when Christ your Redeemer will say, "You stewarded your life well by aspiring to do good toward all people"? Do you confirm your membership among God's elect by devoting your time to meeting the obvious and urgent needs around you so as not to be unfruitful? The exchange of greetings at the end of this letter admonishes us to ask such questions so that we might have true assurance of our conversion.

Prayer

Mighty Creator and Redeemer, thank you for revealing to me how my disposition towards philanthropy reflects my disposition toward you. To believe in you and belong to your people means I should be zealous for good works. Free me from the belief that abounding in good is an option for some believers or a way of life limited to particular seasons of life. Move me, now, from understanding to action. Amen.

Day 25

Titus 3:15

"All who are with me greet you.
Greet those who love us in the faith.
Grace be with you all."

PAUL BEGAN THIS LETTER by wishing "grace and peace from God the Father and Christ Jesus our Savior" (1:4). So now he concludes the letter with the blessing, "Grace be with you all." The strategic placement of these prayers of grace reminds us that all of life is rooted in and driven by grace.

"Grace" has different nuances in the New Testament. In this letter it refers to God's empowerment so that his people can obey him (1:4; 3:15). It's also used to describe Christ's first appearance (2:11). Finally, it expresses God's motivation in saving sinners (3:7). But perhaps the best way to understand grace is by highlighting its divine and dynamic quality: as recipients of the Father's favor in Christ, we are to extend grace to all, so that all might see and glorify him. Paul's final prayer in 3:15 is that believers would pursue good works out of a knowledge and experience of God's abiding grace in their own lives.

How can we do this? Jesus taught: "I am the vine; you are the branches. Whoever abides in me and I in him, he it is that bears much fruit, for apart from me you can do nothing" (John 15:5). If we try to obey God out of our own resources, we will grow weary and disheartened. Jesus could not be clearer that we are deficient in of ourselves and are therefore in desperate need of his empowering grace. Thus, we must abide in him. But how, someone might ask, do we abide in Christ? For the typical evangelical Christian, this amounts to a robust devotional life that entails Bible meditation and prayer. In no way am I dismissing the necessity and goodness of such spiritual disciplines. But it's noteworthy that the Letter to Titus ends on the note, "Grace be with you *all*." There is no place for the lone ranger Christians (see especially Titus 2:1–10). God's empowering grace to do good is received when we abide in Christ; and we abide in Christ when we dwell among his people.

Too often believers are stirred by the call to do good and go out on their own to change the world. But Paul has made clear that Christ's work of redemption brings us into his family. This closing prayer of blessing reminds us both of our need for grace and its source.

Prayer

God, give me grace to do the good works you have prepared for me in advance. And thank you for making that grace available through the communion of saints. In my desire to do good, protect me from autonomy. Instead, teach me to rely on you by integrating myself fully into your people. Amen.

Summary

I GREW UP IN a church context that underscored personal piety, expressed especially in a rich devotional life marked by Bible reading and prayer. But little emphasis, if any, was ever put on pursuing good. At best, I was taught to serve in the church, but little was ever said of pursuing philanthropy. All in all, my spiritual life was marked by isolationism: church buildings functioned as fortresses to protect us from all the evils lurking around, and church programs were designed to keep us out of trouble.

Any evangelistic effort tended to focus on "word" versus "deed." That is, we learned the scripts, embodied especially in "The Four Spiritual Laws." We even read books that addressed typical issues and challenges related to the Christian faith. But, again, little emphasis was ever placed on developing deep relationships with unbelievers or pursuing a life marked by good works toward all people. Perhaps the exceptions were vocational missionaries that sought to apply their unique skills to enhancing society. But even this seemed confined to the select few "super" believers.

The more I studied the Bible, however, I found this absence not just surprising but also unsettling. Repeatedly, as we have touched upon in this devotional, the New Testament underscores the role that good works play in declaring the kingdom of God and advancing the gospel. I sometimes wonder if the church is losing ground not because it is being faithful but because it is falling short of the wholistic call to advance the gospel in word *and* deed. At the risk of unfair generalizations, I find this tendency to be more common especially among believers who are committed to upholding orthodox theology (of which I am very much a fan). With all our effort to maintain the truth of the gospel, I wonder if our gospel-fidelity has become imbalanced through a quiet dismissal of good works as the preoccupation of liberal Christians. I would like to see a recovery of the kind of wholistic spirituality reflected in the Letter to Titus, an embrace of the truth that accords with godliness (1:1). It seems that believers tend to adopt an either-or approach—either to doctrinal precision or to commendable living. Authentic gospel-centered spirituality knows no such dichotomy.

Years ago, John Piper wrote a challenging book *Don't Waste Your Life*. His emphasis on the brevity of life resonated deeply with me. As Piper highlights, too many Christians have drunk the Kool-Aid of coasting through life, living without distinction and purpose. To be clear, we should enjoy everything God has created. But many Christians, at least in the West, don't seem to struggle with this. Their lives equal if not surpass the luxuries and pleasures of their secular colleagues. Paul's point in this letter is not just that life is short but that the first and second coming of Christ demands that we steward life well, particularly in the form of pursuing good works. Our lives are indeed wasted if at the end they have been inconsequential as a result of being drowned out with worldly pursuits: we were saved to engage in philanthropy in order to reflect the great Philanthropist. My hope is that this devotional has facilitated some conviction that our life should very much be about good works—not in order to be saved but because we have been saved.

The Letter to Titus suggests difficult but important personal questions: "Am I a believer? Do I belong to the people of God?" Like a good pastor, Paul never sought to create unnecessary doubt. I'm not sure if his intention was even to make us unduly introspective. His main concern seemed to be with unwarranted confidence in one's conversion even in the absence of good works. Paul could not be clearer in this letter: if your life is devoid of good works, if you lack zeal to do good toward all, you should wonder whether you have ever encountered *the* Philanthropist. Of course it isn't the case that if your life is marked by philanthropy, then you must be a Christian. But if your life is deficient of both good works and a desire to do good, this letter challenges you to ask whether you're all that different from the false teachers who make a show of their allegiance to God but ultimately deny him by their works (1:16).

I recognize the inherent and unending danger of falling back into the belief that my good works in some shape or form contribute to my salvation. Therefore, I want to be emphatic by echoing Paul's own words that God saved us not because of works done by us in righteousness but because of his own kindness and mercy (3:5). This gospel declaration must be made loudly and repeatedly in our lives because of the persistent and malicious voice that says, "Look at the good you've done—surely God must bless you as a result." Both this devotional and Paul's letter adamantly reject "works-righteousness," the idea that our works merit God's favor.

Still, Paul says without hesitation and with all authority that a genuine Christian should abound in good. If by reading this devotional you have begun to wonder what the absence of good works in your life might suggest, don't begin by stapling the fruit of good works into your life. Apart from being organically connected to the tree of life, they will fall and perish. The more basic step is to ask whether you are in Christ. Sure, you may have been raised in the church and are therefore well-versed in the Bible stories. Perhaps you went to seminary or even teach at a seminary. But none of this means that you have truly converted, especially if the absence of the fruit of Christ's Spirit becomes more evident as you ponder over Titus. One basic purpose of this letter is to get us to ask the hard question, "Do I possess true faith, a faith that embraces Christ and bears fruit in philanthropy?"

A final point I want to reiterate is that good works, like anything else in the Christian life, require intentionality. That is, good intentions alone will not get the job done. This principle holds true for all of life; and thus we apply it to the things we care about. If we wish to master a language, we must be intentional about carving out regular time each day to learning vocabulary and bumbling through the language. If we wish to purchase a home, we must be careful to set aside enough money for a number of years to make the down payment. Individuals and companies that get things done tend to set SMART goals. But this practice is simply an application of the more general principle of being purposeful.

For many, because philanthropy is so foreign, a life devoted to good will require that much more intentionality. For some, it may take the form of mechanically budgeting time and money for the sole purpose of doing good: "This year we will give two percent of our money away to the various outreach initiatives at our church." "We reserve Wednesday nights to connecting with our neighbor." "We resolve to go on one less vacation so that the family can participate in a service project." Given our culture's obsession with authenticity, such intentionality might not seem all that appealing. It might feel "forced" or "insincere." I suggest disregarding such sentiments. Almost all good things in life require mechanical devotion. The bottom line is that if we are serious about devoting ourselves to doing good, we must be purposeful especially about the ways we spend our time and money.

One additional area that requires intentionality—and we have highlighted this already in the devotional—relates to the company we keep. This book is dedicated to my dear friends Paul and Bora. There are few individuals who better embody intentionality and philanthropy. When I think of them, I'm almost filled with envy over how much the Lord must delight in their lives. I sometimes wonder if they sleep at all because their lives are much like that of Dorcus who was always attending to the needs of everyone around her (Acts 9:36). Their presence and ministry to so many have infected countless people to aspire to good works. If I can illustrate their lives, they are trailblazers in doing good, leaving a tremendous example for their sons and for all the saints.

We all need such people in life if we desire to do good. We need people who deepen our understanding of the great Philanthropist by pursuing the good with a transcendent zeal. As noted in the last devotion, God's grace for us to pursue philanthropy will depend in large part on our community of faith. I pray that you will pursue people whose love for God and zeal for good will spur you on in your effort to bring glory to the Father by abounding in good.

Bibliography

Bonhoeffer, Dietrich. *The Cost of Discipleship*. New York: Touchstone, 1959.

Butterfield, Rosaria. *The Gospel Comes with a House Key: Practicing Radically Ordinary Hospitality in Our Post-Christian World*. Wheaton, IL: Crossway, 2018.

DeYoung, Kevin. *Crazy Busy: A (Mercifully) Short Book about a (Really) Big Problem*. Wheaton, IL: Crossway, 2013.

Jeon, Paul S. *God's Wisdom for Making Peace: Daily Devotions in the Letter to Philemon*. Eugene, OR: Resource, 2018.

———. *A New King: Encountering the Risen Son*. Eugene, OR: Wipf & Stock, 2018.

———. *To Exhort and Reprove: Audience Response to the Chiastic Structures of Paul's Letter to Titus*. Eugene, OR: Pickwick, 2012.

———. *True Faith: Reflections on Paul's Letter to Titus*. Eugene, OR: Wipf & Stock, 2012.

Keller, Timothy. *Counterfeit Gods: The Empty Promises of Money, Sex, and Power, and the Only Hope that Matters*. New York: Dutton, 2009.

———. *Ministries of Mercy: The Call of the Jericho Road*. Third edition. Phillipsburg, NJ: P&R, 2015.

———. *The Reason for God: Belief in an Age of Skepticism*. New York: Dutton, 2008.

Knight, Phil. *Shoe Dog: A Memoir by the Creator of NIKE*. New York: Simon & Schuster, 2016.

Lewis, C. S. *Mere Christianity*. New York: HarperOne, 1980.

McKeown, Greg. *Essentialism: The Disciplined Pursuit of Less*. New York: Crown Business, 2014.

Morgan, Tony. *The Unstuck Church: Equipping Churches to Experience Sustained Health*. Nashville, TN: Thomas Nelson, 2017.

Newport, Cal. *Deep Work: Rules for Focused Success in a Distracted World*. New York: Grand Central, 2016.

Piper, John. *Don't Waste Your Life*. Wheaton, IL: Crossway, 2007.

Rainer, Thom S., and Eric Geiger. *Simple Church: Returning to God's Process for Making Disciples*. Nashville, TN: B&H, 2011.

Towner, Philip H. *The Letters to Timothy and Titus*. New International Greek Testament Commentary. Grand Rapids: Eerdmans, 2006.

Vance, J. D. *Hillbilly Elegy: A Memoir of a Family and Culture in Crisis*. New York: HarperCollins, 2016.

Walls, Jeannette. *The Glass Castle: A Memoir*. New York: Scribner, 2005.

Westover, Tara. *Educated: A Memoir*. New York: Random House, 2018.

Witherington III, Ben. *Letters and Homilies for Hellenized Christians, Vol. 1: A Socio-Rhetorical Commentary on Titus, 1–2 Timothy and 1–3 John*. Downers Grove, IL: IVP Academic, 2006.

CPSIA information can be obtained
at www.ICGtesting.com
Printed in the USA
FFHW011311221119
56071616-62080FF